BY

CHECKERBOARD PRESS ❖ NEW YORK

Copyright © 1991 Checkerboard Press, Inc. All rights reserved.
ISBN: 1-56288-197-3 Printed in the United States of America
0 9 8 7 6 5 4 3 2 1 (B/1/1)

DINOSAURS FOREVER!!

Gus is traveling through time in his time machine. His first stop is the prehistoric era. See if you can find Gus, and also look for:

- Artist
- Back float
- Barbecue grill
- Beach ball
- Book
- 3 Campfires
- Cars
- Chain-link fence
- 2 Coconuts
- Dentist
- 5 Dinosaur eggs
- Diver
- Dog bone
- 2 Ducks
- 2 Fish
- Fishing pole
- Flowers
- Football helmets
- Frying pan
- Giant footprint
- Guitar
- 4 Hats
- Ladder
- Leash
- 2 Lions
- Magnifying glass
- Mammoth
- Mountain climber
- Nut
- 3 Palm trees
- Raft
- Ringmaster
- Ring of sharks
- Saddle
- Sand castle
- 2 Shopping bags
- Shovel and pail
- Skeleton
- Sore toe
- Spatula
- 2 Suitcases
- Sunrise
- Surfer
- Toolbox
- Toothaches
- Torch
- Toy sailboat
- Volcano
- Whale
- … and lots more!

The place is Ancient Greece, and the very first Olympic Games are underway. Gus arrives in time to leap into the competition. Can you find Gus and:

○ Anteater
○ Baby carriage
○ Baseball mitt
○ Bass fiddle
○ Batter
○ Beach ball
○ Bird's nest
○ Bowling ball
○ Boxers
○ 2 Camels
○ Camera
○ Cat
○ Cheerleaders
○ Conductor
○ 3 Cows
○ Discus
○ Dog leash
○ Drums
○ Elephant
○ Finish line
○ Flower
○ Flute
○ Football players
○ Giraffe
○ 3 Goats

○ Greyhounds
○ Harp
○ Hippopotamus
○ Hotdogs
○ 2 Hula-Hoops
○ Javelin throwers
○ Lawn mower
○ Long jump
○ Microphone
○ Motorcycle
○ Ostrich
○ Pelican
○ Police barrier
○ Rabbit
○ 3 Sheep
○ Starting pistol
○ TV camera
○ Tennis racket
○ Ticket window
○ Tuba
○ Turkey
○ Unicycle
○ 2 Weight lifters
○ William
...and lots more!

Gus is at the Colosseum in Ancient Rome. He wants to look around the city before he goes inside to watch the show. Find Gus and:

- Arm wrestlers
- Bricks
- Brush
- Canopy
- Cat
- Cheerleader
- Chef's hat
- Chicken
- Crown of laurels
- Dogsled
- Elephants
- Fountain
- Green hat
- Hard hat
- Headphones
- Hearts
- Inflatable raft
- Kangaroo
- 3 Lions
- Luggage
- 6 Mice
- Orator
- Pelican
- Pizza
- Police barriers
- Puddle
- Pumpkin
- Purple umbrella
- Red Cross
- Rosie
- Rowboat
- Running dog
- Sail
- Sedan
- 3 Shovels
- Spear
- Stop sign
- Swimmer
- Thumbs-up
- Tie salesman
- Trash can
- Trophy
- Wagon
- Waiter
- Walking staff
- Water glass
- Wheelbarrow
- 3 Whips
- William
- Winged horse
- Winner

... and lots more!

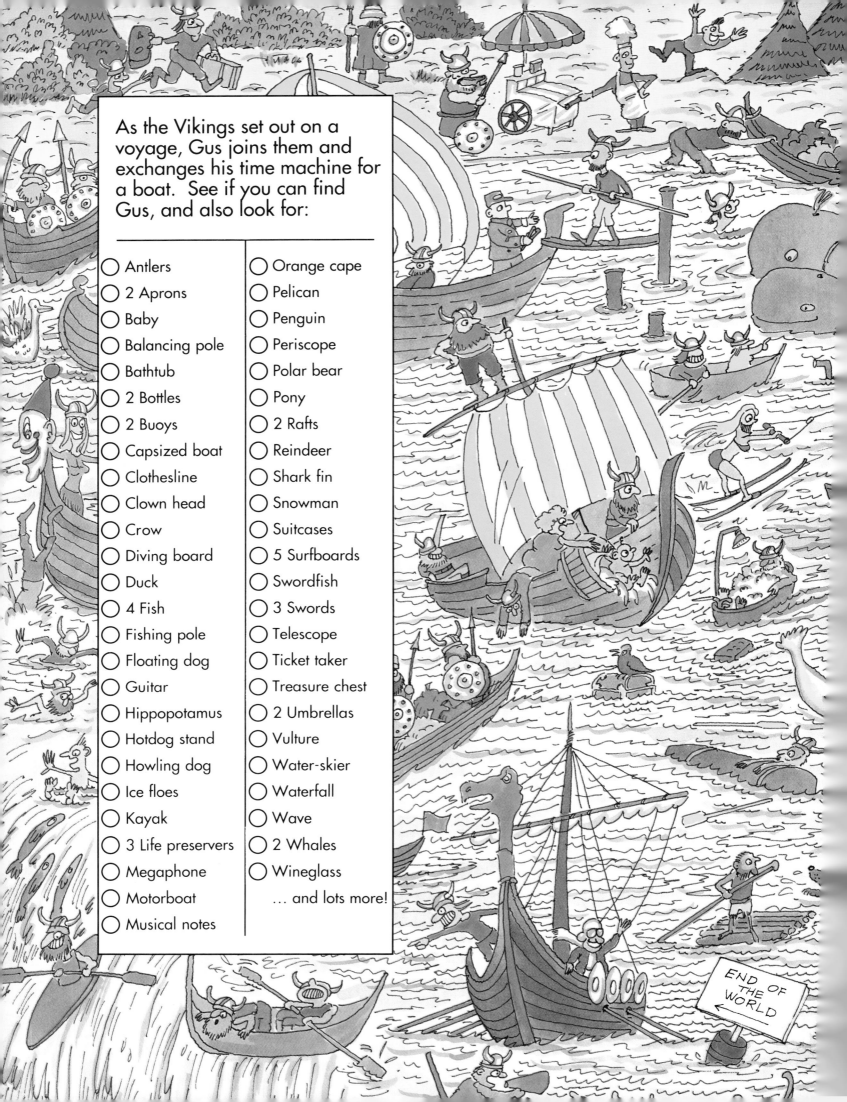

As the Vikings set out on a voyage, Gus joins them and exchanges his time machine for a boat. See if you can find Gus, and also look for:

- Antlers
- 2 Aprons
- Baby
- Balancing pole
- Bathtub
- 2 Bottles
- 2 Buoys
- Capsized boat
- Clothesline
- Clown head
- Crow
- Diving board
- Duck
- 4 Fish
- Fishing pole
- Floating dog
- Guitar
- Hippopotamus
- Hotdog stand
- Howling dog
- Ice floes
- Kayak
- 3 Life preservers
- Megaphone
- Motorboat
- Musical notes
- Orange cape
- Pelican
- Penguin
- Periscope
- Polar bear
- Pony
- 2 Rafts
- Reindeer
- Shark fin
- Snowman
- Suitcases
- 5 Surfboards
- Swordfish
- 3 Swords
- Telescope
- Ticket taker
- Treasure chest
- 2 Umbrellas
- Vulture
- Water-skier
- Waterfall
- Wave
- 2 Whales
- Wineglass
- … and lots more!

END OF THE WORLD

Gus has never been to a fair like this one. It is the Middle Ages, and he is having lots of fun. Find Gus, and also look for:

_____

- Acrobats
- Alligator
- Archer
- Balloon
- 2 Baskets
- 2 Battering rams
- 2 Bikinis
- Bird cage
- Blacksmith
- Broom
- Bull's-eye
- Camel
- Cow
- Diving board
- Drawbridge
- Ducks
- Executioner
- Falcon
- Fishing pole
- Flowers
- Goat
- Hippopotamus
- 4 Horseshoes
- Hotdog stand
- Hula-Hoop
- Inflatable raft

- Jousting knights
- Juggler
- Ladder
- Life preserver
- Mail carrier
- Mandolin
- Moat
- 2 Pennants
- Pie wagon
- Pig
- Police officer
- Rapunzel
- Rat
- Referee
- Sailboat
- Shovel
- Stilts
- Stocks
- Telescope
- Town crier
- Trained bear
- Traveling players
- Turkey
- Wheelbarrow
- … and lots more!

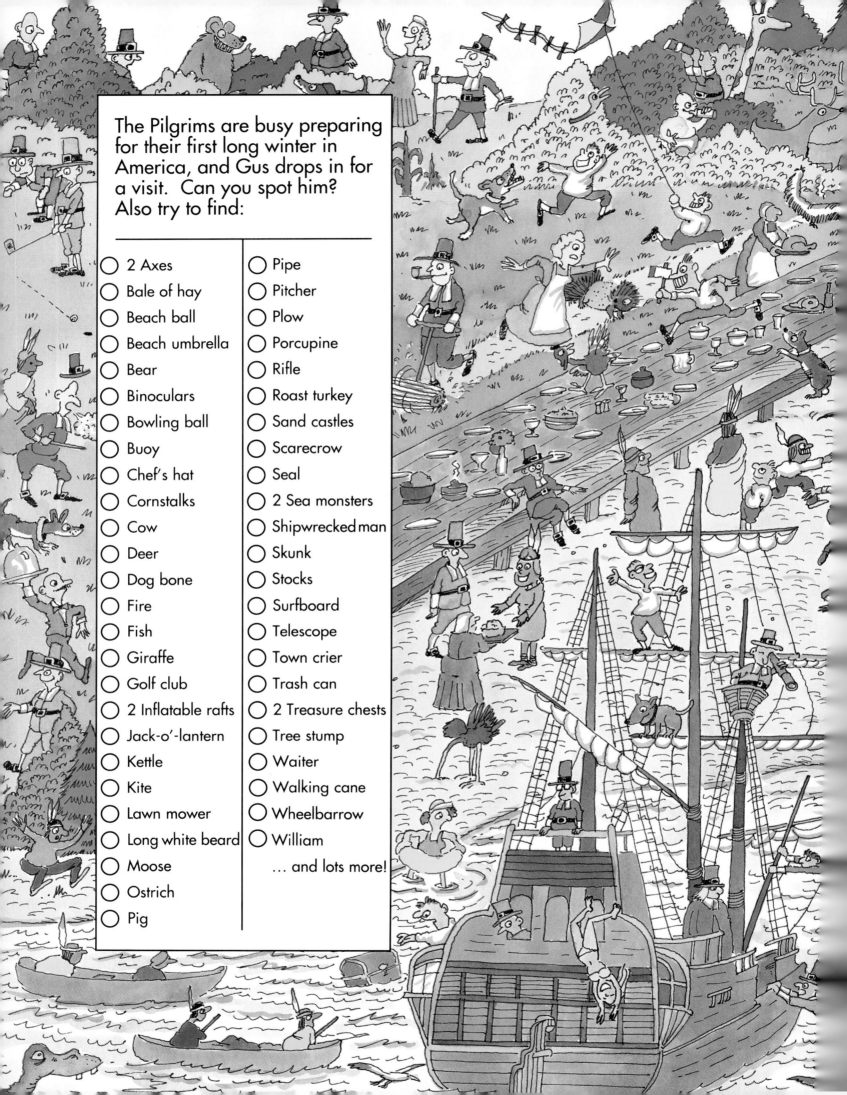

The Pilgrims are busy preparing for their first long winter in America, and Gus drops in for a visit. Can you spot him? Also try to find:

- 2 Axes
- Bale of hay
- Beach ball
- Beach umbrella
- Bear
- Binoculars
- Bowling ball
- Buoy
- Chef's hat
- Cornstalks
- Cow
- Deer
- Dog bone
- Fire
- Fish
- Giraffe
- Golf club
- 2 Inflatable rafts
- Jack-o'-lantern
- Kettle
- Kite
- Lawn mower
- Long white beard
- Moose
- Ostrich
- Pig
- Pipe
- Pitcher
- Plow
- Porcupine
- Rifle
- Roast turkey
- Sand castles
- Scarecrow
- Seal
- 2 Sea monsters
- Shipwrecked man
- Skunk
- Stocks
- Surfboard
- Telescope
- Town crier
- Trash can
- 2 Treasure chests
- Tree stump
- Waiter
- Walking cane
- Wheelbarrow
- William
- ... and lots more!

It's 1849 and the great California Gold Rush has just started. Gus thinks that a gold nugget would make a great souvenir. Try to find Gus and:

- Alligator
- Awning
- 2 Barrels
- Bathtub
- 2 Bears
- Boardwalk
- Bow and arrows
- 5 Bubbles
- 4 Buffalo
- 2 Cacti
- Camera
- 2 Campfires
- Canoe
- Cave
- Chain gang
- Chimney
- Coonskin hat
- Covered wagon
- Cow skull
- Dinosaur
- Doghouse
- Dynamite
- Eagle
- Flag
- Flashlight
- Knapsack
- Knight
- 2 Log cabins
- Monk
- Moose
- Mummy
- Parking meter
- Peg leg
- Plunger
- Pot of gold
- Rabbit
- 2 Rifles
- Rocking chair
- St. Bernard dog
- Sheriff
- 2 Spears
- Stagecoach
- Stirrup
- Stocks
- Sword
- Target
- Tent
- Viking
- Violin
- Watermelon
- Well

...and lots more!

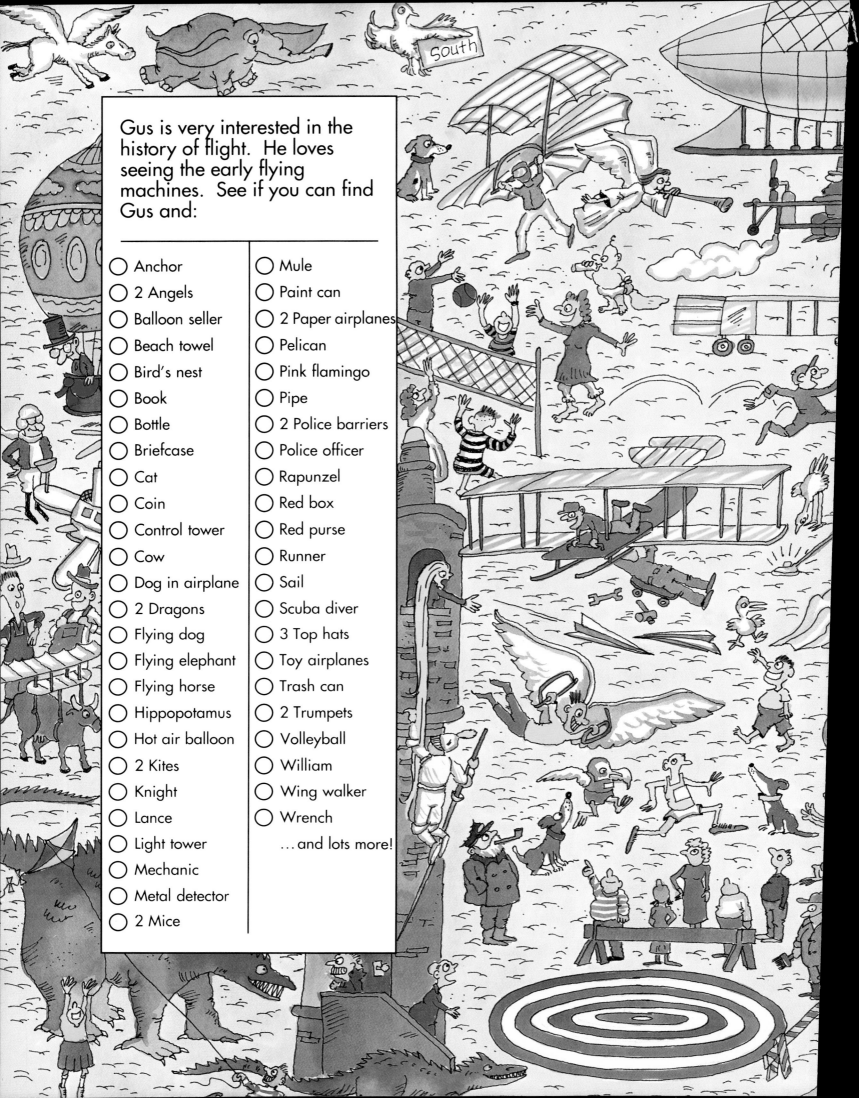

Gus is very interested in the history of flight. He loves seeing the early flying machines. See if you can find Gus and:

- Anchor
- 2 Angels
- Balloon seller
- Beach towel
- Bird's nest
- Book
- Bottle
- Briefcase
- Cat
- Coin
- Control tower
- Cow
- Dog in airplane
- 2 Dragons
- Flying dog
- Flying elephant
- Flying horse
- Hippopotamus
- Hot air balloon
- 2 Kites
- Knight
- Lance
- Light tower
- Mechanic
- Metal detector
- 2 Mice
- Mule
- Paint can
- 2 Paper airplanes
- Pelican
- Pink flamingo
- Pipe
- 2 Police barriers
- Police officer
- Rapunzel
- Red box
- Red purse
- Runner
- Sail
- Scuba diver
- 3 Top hats
- Toy airplanes
- Trash can
- 2 Trumpets
- Volleyball
- William
- Wing walker
- Wrench

...and lots more!

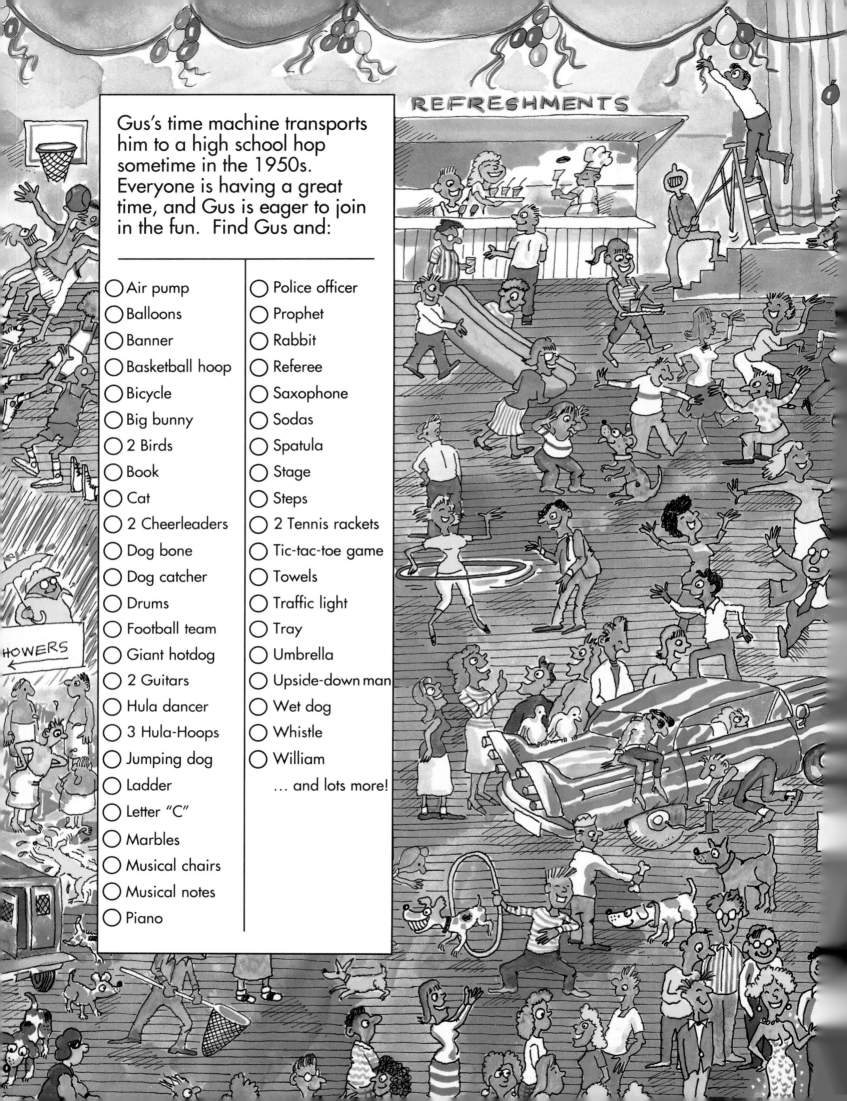

Gus's time machine transports him to a high school hop sometime in the 1950s. Everyone is having a great time, and Gus is eager to join in the fun. Find Gus and:

- Air pump
- Balloons
- Banner
- Basketball hoop
- Bicycle
- Big bunny
- 2 Birds
- Book
- Cat
- 2 Cheerleaders
- Dog bone
- Dog catcher
- Drums
- Football team
- Giant hotdog
- 2 Guitars
- Hula dancer
- 3 Hula-Hoops
- Jumping dog
- Ladder
- Letter "C"
- Marbles
- Musical chairs
- Musical notes
- Piano

- Police officer
- Prophet
- Rabbit
- Referee
- Saxophone
- Sodas
- Spatula
- Stage
- Steps
- 2 Tennis rackets
- Tic-tac-toe game
- Towels
- Traffic light
- Tray
- Umbrella
- Upside-down man
- Wet dog
- Whistle
- William

… and lots more!

REFRESHMENTS

HOWERS

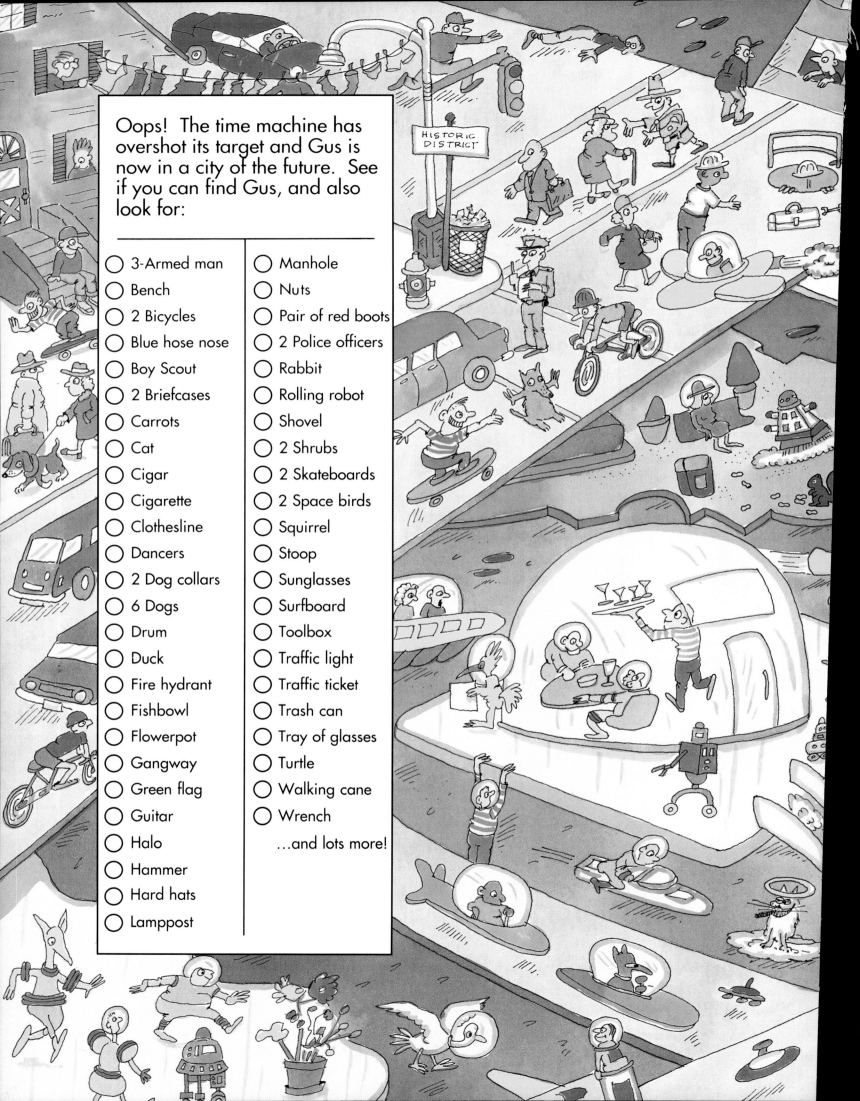

Oops! The time machine has overshot its target and Gus is now in a city of the future. See if you can find Gus, and also look for:

- 3-Armed man
- Bench
- 2 Bicycles
- Blue hose nose
- Boy Scout
- 2 Briefcases
- Carrots
- Cat
- Cigar
- Cigarette
- Clothesline
- Dancers
- 2 Dog collars
- 6 Dogs
- Drum
- Duck
- Fire hydrant
- Fishbowl
- Flowerpot
- Gangway
- Green flag
- Guitar
- Halo
- Hammer
- Hard hats
- Lamppost
- Manhole
- Nuts
- Pair of red boots
- 2 Police officers
- Rabbit
- Rolling robot
- Shovel
- 2 Shrubs
- 2 Skateboards
- 2 Space birds
- Squirrel
- Stoop
- Sunglasses
- Surfboard
- Toolbox
- Traffic light
- Traffic ticket
- Trash can
- Tray of glasses
- Turtle
- Walking cane
- Wrench
- ...and lots more!

HISTORIC DISTRICT

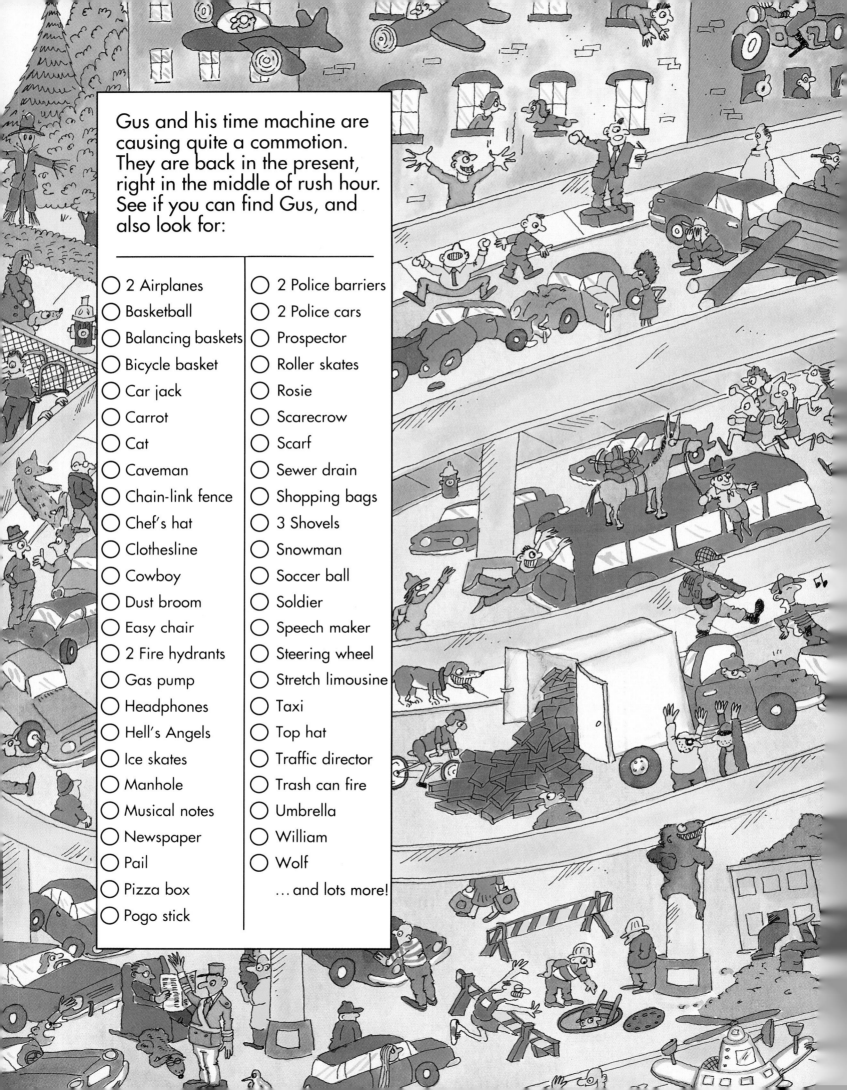

Gus and his time machine are causing quite a commotion. They are back in the present, right in the middle of rush hour. See if you can find Gus, and also look for:

- 2 Airplanes
- Basketball
- Balancing baskets
- Bicycle basket
- Car jack
- Carrot
- Cat
- Caveman
- Chain-link fence
- Chef's hat
- Clothesline
- Cowboy
- Dust broom
- Easy chair
- 2 Fire hydrants
- Gas pump
- Headphones
- Hell's Angels
- Ice skates
- Manhole
- Musical notes
- Newspaper
- Pail
- Pizza box
- Pogo stick

- 2 Police barriers
- 2 Police cars
- Prospector
- Roller skates
- Rosie
- Scarecrow
- Scarf
- Sewer drain
- Shopping bags
- 3 Shovels
- Snowman
- Soccer ball
- Soldier
- Speech maker
- Steering wheel
- Stretch limousine
- Taxi
- Top hat
- Traffic director
- Trash can fire
- Umbrella
- William
- Wolf
- … and lots more!

Now that Gus is back in his own time, the time machine has found its own place in history — at the museum! Look for Gus and:

- ○ Alarm clock
- ○ Backpack
- ○ Beach ball
- ○ Bench
- ○ Bicycle
- ○ Broom
- ○ Camera
- ○ Cash register
- ○ Caveman
- ○ Diver
- ○ Dragon's tail
- ○ Frying pan
- ○ 3 Guards
- ○ Guitar
- ○ Hand truck
- ○ Harness
- ○ Ice cream cone
- ○ Information booth
- ○ Lucy
- ○ Open book
- ○ Postcards
- ○ Roller skates
- ○ Shopping bag
- ○ Sleeping cat
- ○ Steps
- ○ Sundae
- ○ Teddy bear
- ○ Television
- ○ Tire
- ○ Trash can
- … and lots more!